BRAIN DEAD

REGGIE JOHNSON

BRAIN DEAD

Copyright © 2017 Reggie Johnson/Rad Press Publishing
Cover Design by: Mitch Green
All rights reserved. No part of this publication may be reproduced, distributed or conveyed without the permission of the publisher.

First printing 2017

REGGIE JOHNSON

PRELUDE

The brain works in mysterious ways. I was always interested in how the brain works to process information. Just like the four sections of the brain, this book is meant to be categorized in four parts: occipital, frontal, parietal, temporal. As you read see how the writing in each section differs and compares to give you an insight of how this brain works. This information overload will leave you brain dead.

OCCIPITAL

REGGIE JOHNSON

"We rely too much on what our eyes see. Looks can be deceiving"

BRAIN DEAD

POLISH

Polished conversations
Dirty mouth won't you get you far, but a pack of Orbitz gum
We're fed the standards and normality of everyday life
That sometimes we get lost in it
No more individuality
There's a time and place for everything
But, who has the place and time for anything?
I just want the time or place since it's something
Some things don't happen that way

REGGIE JOHNSON

TEARS

Water precipitates from the eyelids
As the damn has been broken by your damn foolishness
Tears? I thought this was a flash flood
Because this came out of nowhere
Just like if we went nowhere fast
And you never said you wanted to take things slow
Like you ever knew that's what despacito meant in English
We got lost in translation numerous times
But these hands in minutes clocked hours and hours of sentimental
conversation that I never could get back
I shared that with you out of confidence
Now it's like I lack that very thing
I can't move on
Or is just my mind telling me not to?
I don't know...

BRAIN DEAD

SILENCE

We have the right to feel what we feel
Just like we have the right to remain silent
Since anything we say or do can be used against us
This innate feeling came from something
A causality that you created
That attachment created a disconnect
If only we could treat it like a dropped call
Then maybe you receive the message

TORCH

When I saw you, my eyes became a flip book of all the memories we had together. If only I had a lighter to torch certain pages and watch the ashes fade away into thin air. Or even if the whole book burns, I'll be fine. At least I got a good read just once that I'll never forget.

BRAIN DEAD

NOTE TO SELF

Do you ever think?
Why do I even bother...
to please you at all?

OPEN

I'm a be honest...
The word open comes to mind when you are confiding in me
Entrusting me with sincerities that you want to keep between you and me
The word open is what we use when we want our minds to formulate our own opinion or view for something new
The word open is used for how I want them legs to be in my peripheral view
Never has it been used to describe a relationship
That's new boundaries...
New territories...
New conversations...
New insecurities...
New experiences...
When all we wanted to do is be old fashioned

BRAIN DEAD

THE RACE

It takes a toll on me...
When you ride our friendship around in circles
If I wanted to see laps, I would watch a NASCAR race
Instead of seeing ours go nowhere
At times, I really just want to wave the checkered flag
If I don't have trust in someone, it's hard for me to get it back
As if you stabbed me in the back and you want to have it
Now it's an awkward feeling sometimes and I can't shake it
Becoming numb to the situation word to Linkin Park
A depreciated foundation, bound to crack down from the start

FRIEND

If I open up to you and consider you a friend
It means I invested enough to give the sixth letter of the alphabet about you
If there is any question about our friendship, we were never friends to begin with
Leaves us wondering what the hell we've been doing all of this time?
And we think why can't we walk away from these individuals?
This toxic bond that somehow, we enjoy being here

BRAIN DEAD

INDULGE

Seeds implanted in soils of the forbidden fruit of our mind
Awakening new life into areas of unknown territories
Unconquered territories...
Precipitation from the worries and nervousness
Enough to irrigate the nerves
This feeling...
Anxious to know what's to come into fruition
Will you indulge?

REGGIE JOHNSON

THE L WORD

I've seen love found in a hopeless place
And love lost just as fluid as time or space
The infamous L word...
And all of the consequences that come from it
Both being in it and falling out of it
I've had the displeasure of experiencing both
I thought love was supposed to be forever
And not heartbreak
One shouldn't continuously open up their heart up like a book
I just want someone to take it off the shelf and keep it
Is it that too much to ask?

BRAIN DEAD

NOTE TO SELF II

When I look back on my life...

I want to see it in various ways

The lessons I learned...

The path I led by example

The accomplishments I've earned

Everything else that doesn't have meaning

It's because there wasn't a word I could curate to make it of value

REGGIE JOHNSON

MOTIVES

If we have to question one's motives
Then, what are we even doing?
Why are we wasting time?
Why we borrowing each other's emotions thinking you have the audacity to lend a helping hand in how the hell I'm supposed to feel about myself?
Was that a mouthful?
Seems like you been giving me an earful
And it's hard to digest...
Just ready to throw my hands up and call it done
When it comes to numbers, this time I'm not the one

BRAIN DEAD

ASYLUM

I solemnly swear I'm up to no good
If I'm worrying about the same things
Over and over again
Hair thinning because they winning
Mind on DJ because it stays spinning
Only request is that it's time for a change
So, empty out your wallets
That I could see the lint in your pockets
Tired of being too plugged in, time to unplug me from the sockets

REGGIE JOHNSON

LOSING MYSELF

Eating me up...
How quickly I tell myself that I'm good
When things aren't that at all
Yet I keep going with the flow
And then I remember how I really feel
Envious of someone that couldn't give a care in the world for me
Even if I was holding it on my shoulders
They add more insult to injury
I'm tired of losing myself in you
I've been missing me

BRAIN DEAD

FRIGHT

Are you afraid of the dark?
Buried under your pillows
When you could've been above ground with me
Could've shown you the light
But I'll let you continues to see the dark skies
All those whispers
Monsters in the wall
Will you be there if I fall?
And if you die because of this, will you let me be your immortal?

REGGIE JOHNSON

DEVIL MAY CRY

The devil may cry

Dante himself wouldn't be ready for the amount of demons I've seen in my lifetime

I wouldn't either...

When they behave in a believable way

Human, yet naïve

Willing to extend an olive branch if you lend a helping hand

But the limb becomes limp and finally breaks

And they don't show any effort trying to repair any relationship with you

They've got what they've needed and now they're gone

But before they leave, the demons unveil their true identities and to my surprise

They turn out to be some of my friends

BRAIN DEAD

TWO FACED

Yourself lands on both sides of the coin
There's no referee to choose who siding with me
Feeling some type a way about me guess you going against the wind
I took too many losses, you content with how you win
How you put up with yourself when you grin?
Just like all good things, so many friendships had to come to an end
Two faced, who needs Batman when you got villains like these?
Flip a coin on your own time
Do as you please...

REGGIE JOHNSON

IN YOUR PHONE
(Inspired by in Your Phone by Ty Dolla $ign & Lauren Juaregui)

You always in your phone

And that's a letdown to me

Your cellular getting more action to me

Steady with them fingers when you got from me

Could've got these hands

They had plans…

Wanted to supply what you demand

Now you left me with my hand

Guess my pain was your pleasure

I feel like you do me wrong, no scale could measure

HALLOW'S EVE

Some people like dressing up in costumes
Since they like hiding who they are
Their innards eat away at the guilt of not being able to look themselves in the eye
And ask themselves "Do I like the person I've become?"
There's not a treat given for tricking us with a façade
Two of hours of going door to door is not enough
Smashing a pumpkin may help get out that frustration you have
Happy Hallow's Eve, you deserve to be bad

REGGIE JOHNSON

DOUBT

Doubting me is the biggest form of flattery

Let my actions be my strength to have you up there feeling weak in the knees

Now that's SWV

So, yield to this red octagon, S.T.O.P.

Only one that can judge me

Is my G.O.D.

BRAIN DEAD

THE WAY LIFE GOES

(Inspired by The Way Life Goes by Lil' Uzi Vert & Nicki Minaj)

There are winners, there are losers

There are beggars, there are choosers

There are people shooting they shots, think they balling Indiana Hoosiers

But I'm from Ohio though

There's people I've supported and they won't even look at my bio though

The way life goes

Just roll with the punches

Coach say to bob and weave, mainly in the crunches

Some people won't fit where you expect, they didn't put in time for their crunches

I could go on a rant and burn some calories

Instead I turn the stress into a salary

Turn a salary into a lifestyle

A lifestyle into a passion

A passion till the end

My ink is everlasting

And I know it hurts sometimes, but I'll get over it

I have another life to live

I know that I'll get over it

NOTE TO SELF III

People never cease to amaze me
We all create preconceived notions about people
That becomes a direct causality to how you interact with them
They initially behave in one way just as you predicted
Then, it only takes one time for them to surprise you
Gives you a new outlook about them
We do this all the time
We say never judge a book by the cover but sometimes we never make it pass the preface
If only we could read between the lines all the time

RAIN

Rain falls like your emotions

Onto the seeds, I implanted into your mind that I did you wrong

I didn't make you cry, if you think so it wasn't on purpose

And when it rains, it pours

You do thunderous actions and I can see the lightening coming from you as begin to scream

A permanent rain cloud you put over my head

Never to see the sun again until I treat you better

Whether I want to do it or not, it's my choice

I'll just have to withstand the weather

REGGIE JOHNSON

CUES

We see sometimes what we want to see
We hear only key words or phrases that make us go through phases of dealing with consequences that a normal troubled heart faces
We are sometimes afraid to speak rationally so through irrational actions we get our point across
All of these things equate to the world we live in
I usually don't do this, speak my mind on current events
But when the events currently have me sometimes afraid to do anything let alone misbehave
Everything we see nowadays is mass shooting in this place, natural disaster in that place
And most of us across the country sit around with a sad face
All of us living afraid of what's going to happen next
I hope we can turn a new leaf soon while we continue to be perplexed

GROWTH

Growth

These moments in our life when we feel like we had to level up

We faced adversaries

Some easy, some kind of scary

We all do differently and results may vary

And when we get to the end, we feel accomplished

For awhile...

Then it seems like things relapse

Fall backwards after moving forward so much

That can be by events, choice of friends

Cause and effect, being a means to an end

And we wonder when will it all end

Growth is constant and I learned the hard way too many times that we

just deal with the bullshit as it comes

PARIETAL

"We feel everything good or bad. Why can't it all be good?"

REGGIE JOHNSON

YOU

To some, it's like you can do no wrong
To me, it's like I have to watch what I say
Feel like I cannot be myself at times
And yet we still continue on this game
All to appease you

BRAIN DEAD

SCARS & BANDAGES

When I lost your trust

It was like hari kari was performed on me

All the good times gushed out

Oozing rapidly, every moment bleeding out

Feeling light headed, I couldn't believe it came to this

Everything all out on the floor and all I wanted was some bandages to heal the old wounds

Now the scars remain to remind me daily of how things used to be before

DEATH

I know death is inevitable...
But how come we can't choose who or what we say goodbye to first?
Like certain friendships and relationships
I know we have the opportunity to learn from one another
However, some of these situations, I'm like why do I even bother?
Never should a person make someone cry or evoke emotions so strong

BRAIN DEAD

CHANGING CHANNELS

Sometimes, I wish I could just turn off my brain
It's like someone sitting in front of a TV flicking through channels of emotions
And I feel it all...
Consumption of the masses and it's like I'm the Walking Dead
Waiting for something bad to happen
When I have everything good to be thankful for
It's like I want to color the clouds black and fill it up with water just so I can rain on my own parade sometimes
Is it me causing all of this or did you play a part in it?
Would you ever admit it?

NOTE TO SELF IV

They say friendships and relationships have a seven-year life cycle

What happened to seven being a lucky number?

Static how frequent the dynamics change

The way I look at it

Each person you come into contact with serve a purpose

Either a lesson or an opportunity to grow with or from the person

There's been many a people that come in and out of our lives

And I sit back and think did I have an effect on how our relationship turned out?

Certain people, I know I have

Good or bad

I value each and every one of them equally

And if I could, I would hope to break this inevitable cycle all of us deal with in our lives

Hopefully, we meant something to each other to stay around

HURT

Should've listened
I get it, you're hurt
And I get it, I've hurt you
We created this perfect moment
That most of us caught a glimpse
Not living in the moment, I was living in the past
Guiding my ways in the present
Forecasting how I'm going to act in the future
I didn't predict the precipitation that would come from the clouds you possess around your eyelids
I only wanted your eyes to glisten like the sun
When it sparkles in the light
But, the light went dark and it was like boogeyman came in and took love away from you
And I didn't do anything to stop it
Or do anything to fight for it
I basically should've just handed you the red balloon
And you would've just called me a clown and got this over with
Hit me all of your rotten tomatoes and I would agree with the critics 100%
I'm a box office sellout and I understand now
I couldn't afford your love

REGGIE JOHNSON

LESSONS LEARNED

I've gotten myself involved in numerous things over the years
Most good, some bad
A lot of actions, a lot of consequences
A lot of static situations became dynamic
And I had to get used to the change and grow
And every day, lessons being learned
I realize that people affected by my actions
No matter the extent
And for that I thank you or apologize for everything
Words I should've said a while ago

BRAIN DEAD

HAUNTED

Haunted by old insecurities from days past
Of relationships that ended in which I wanted to make it last
Memories become ghosts as they float around my mind, begging for their vessel to become real life again
But, some just need to fade away
Put ease on my mind, like I once did for you
And let me go, even though I didn't want to do the same for you

REGGIE JOHNSON

WEARY BONES

I can sense the weariness in your bones
You must not have sensed something this real before
It even makes me nervous...
I don't usually be this forward
But, I don't want us to go backwards
I'm tired of the time standing still by myself
I want it to stop when I'm with you
I want to feel the goosebumps when we kiss
And when we watch a scary movie
I want to feel the warmth of our bodies together when we embrace
The flame burns to the core for you
And I just want to say I like you before it's too late

A LITTLE WORK

(Inspired by A Little Work by Fergie)

Got a lot of answers I'm looking for in these words
Writing is what I turn to when I think this shits for the birds
This is for the ones that gave me the curve
And the ones that had the nerve
To walk out of my life as if I ruined theirs
The ones that said they would be, but didn't end up being there
We all may be broken
We all are just little bit hurt
And we may need a little help
We all need a little work
On one's self

REGGIE JOHNSON

DON'T TAKE IT PERSONAL

(Inspired by Don't Take It Personal by Lyrica Anderson)

Defense mechanism

Seems like when I open up a little, it's like I cause a cataclysm

It's like when I get close to someone, I end up creating a schism

I do this to everyone and I can't help it

Always think I'm going to be let down and for that it's like I'm selfish

Got my guards up, like I'm defending my kingdom

Sorry for being caught up in this sick thing and me treating you like you're a symptom

Don't take it personal

BRAIN DEAD

WIND

I've seen the wind carry people in many directions
With one another, drifting one another
Everything's cool, low pressure
Then something changes in the atmosphere
Causes us to go in different ways
Turbulence masking as high pressure
What caused this weather to go from clear skies to a tornado of destruction?
What will happen when the dust settle?
I have nothing left to give...

REGGIE JOHNSON

WHITE NOISE

They say actions speak louder than words
Silence is anthemic
That white noise resonates in me more harmful than any word in
the dictionary could ever do
Than any physical abuse could ever do
Solo or group effort doesn't matter because you've won best song
of the year
I don't know what I ever did to deserve this the several times
But, this has become my most played track in my mind
And I'm beginning to lose it

BRAIN DEAD

HEART

I wish you could hear what my heart is saying
The soft whisper hasn't caught your ear
It says I want to bend you over this table
Kiss you softly as I raise your shirt
Lick the ink off the tattoo as if my saliva was the ink behind the drawing
Turn you over and kiss you all over
And then...
My mouth begins...
To say, hey how are you doing today?

REGGIE JOHNSON

NIGHTFALL

When night falls

My brain clocks in for work

Third shift duties as it keeps me up late

Serving up some thoughts and I got a lot up on my plate

A lot to digest, some are a hard pill to swallow

Hope it don't make me sick, no pain to follow

You are the boss

Got control over me

And I'm just sitting up here saying

What do you want from me?

BRAIN DEAD

PIECES

All of the pieces used to fit together
Now it's broken and I'm crying out for help
And you smile with no remorse
Might as well laugh at my pain acting like Kevin Hart
Who even knew you had a heartbeat?
I guess we're all comedians
Laughter leads to a healthy life
I thought it was you that made everything right in my life

REGGIE JOHNSON

HUMAN NATURE

Like leaves in the wind...
I began falling for you
And when I fall, I fall hard
I extended my branch to you
Hoping in return that this new journey will be fruitful
But, you cut me off limb by limb until you got what you wanted
Deforest nature as you told me you clear everyone out if they get too close
You should've just through a match at my roots and watch me burn from the ground up
Because that's how I feel
I hope you're happy

BRAIN DEAD

TANGLED WEB

It all started with one statement
We're friends no matter what
The webbing began
And you tangled lie after lie until I believed it to be true
Your actions braided and expanded the web
Snowballing in front of your eyes
And I'm immobilized
Like a moth awaiting to be taking by its predator
Jokes on me for getting caught up believing everything you say

REGGIE JOHNSON

DON'T JUDGE ME
(Inspired by Don't Judge Me by Ty Dolla $ign, Future & Swae Lee)

Lately, I been going through a lot of things
Temporary fix by some drinking
Had to do something different on some quick thinking
Thinking, what was I thinking?
There's sometimes that I feel like I'm sinking
Certain people and events affect me like quick sand
Leaves a bad taste in mouth, all bland
Some new writing is on demand
Just rock with me, it's a simple plan
Simple Plan, no rock band
Simple plan, like a quick scheme
Persevere by any means
Lately, I been going through some things

BRAIN DEAD

ACTIONS

There were a lot of things left unsaid
Left misunderstood
Left covering up the bad
And mistaking all your actions for good
It was some things that was done that had some consequences
At times, we may have been near and dear, but it created for us some distance
It's crazy how quick an opinion of you can change in one instance

QUESTIONS

Something that's always in the back of my mind...
When will I find true love?
Why is there not a set time or age?
I just think...
When I do find it?...
Will life be completely fulfilled?
Or will I just be looking for something else to fill a void I have?

BRAIN DEAD

PRESSURE

I know one thing…
I'm a sure thing…
One day I'm a give you that wedding ring
Right now, you giving me the chastity ring
Want the benefits without being mine
How many times? Yeah, I said how many times?
Times that by your actions
Add in some distractions
And now I'm giving you the satisfaction
Of giving a damn about someone when they got me ready to break
The pressure from the water got me ready for an escape

SOMEBODY

(Inspired by Somebody by Lyrica Anderson)

You gonna see me with somebody...

One day, you gonna be salty...

Peppered in and out of my life, now your body is seasoned on its Lawry's

I'm really over you, that's my mind state

She on her Cavs, I'm on my Golden State

Game 7, Steph Curry

She played me, on some Kyrie, ready to switch up in a hurry

Take your talents to Boston

BRAIN DEAD

WHISKEY FEATURING I. WIMANA C

(Inspired by Whiskey by Maroon 5 & A$AP Rocky)

Temps dropping in October I told you to call me once your sober The hangover's worse once we're older and I waited and waited and waited and waited Then I debated, to be elated if we dated Created my favorites moments in time and savored it But in my mind is where they stayed The only thing drunk love wanted to do was get laid As if it were a transaction, like it was looking to get paid She'll pay for it alright the next morning Sunglasses and Advil, the night before lives in mourning Wake me up in November Hopefully you'll get to remember Me

-Reggie Johnson

Cold bones live in October, I told her after drinks she should come over, Late nights await under the cover, Warmth trickles through bodies as friction sparks ember, Flesh upon flesh screams echo our names, She's riding, heat raises frosting our windowpane, Back bends-it depends, she can arch both ways, No talking, our bodies language expresses all we need to say, Bed creaks, she peaks, wet sheets, knees weak, We crawl, both fall, straight into deep sleep, Morning's light is the first sight gracing our vision, But the show wasn't over, it was just intermission, Press play no more delay, until the rolling of credits, Sweater weather, raw footage, none censored, no edits

-I. Wimana C.

REGGIE JOHNSON

BROKEN FEATURING ANDRE WOODS

Sifting through memories As each one sprinkles a different emotion from the next Either way you make it, she still leaves a bad taste in my mouth My mouth once enjoyed each and every bit of you From the inside and out Sexually and mentally Physically and chemically But in the science of things We ended up being just an experiment Testing the waters The pH levels stood for phony as the relationship became too acidic to maintain We weren't meant for each other And I wanted it to work so bad But my heart gave up And I'm glad it went flatline for your love But I haven't found another person to bring life to it again

-Reggie Johnson

I can feel my love begin to relapse, Toying with the temptation of Lust. Tip toeing to soundless music and scavenging for a song that has already faded to its finish. The chills I once gave you raise along my very own skin and your existence sends me Braille written messages in cold isolated rooms, as I yearn for the human I used to be when we were once we. "We were once we, We were once we, We were once we..." I think that is how the song goes... My heart beats, your feet flea, and again, that is how the high dozed... As my love relapses for a lust you once sang. Art or science, you and I always seemed to end the same way... as I listen to a flat line...

-Andre Woods

TEMPORAL

REGGIE JOHNSON

"We equate feelings to a specific time and place. I just want to remember the good times"

FRED

07/06/15 will be remembered as the day I lost a part of me
The phone calls on the holidays
The gloating to other people as he would tell everyone of how well his grandson is
I didn't get to see him much, but when I did it was always a good time
He always wanted the best for me and I hope he is watching over smiling
Until we meet again, Grandpa

REGGIE JOHNSON

BULLIED

I was in the first or second grade
Getting on the school bus
My mom waves as the bus pulls away
And it was like the longest twenty-minute bus ride
That was when I got picked on, made fun of, laughed at
Continued to happen until my mom got on that bus before it pulled off one day
Told every single kid on that bus that if there's a problem, she'll resolve it
Otherwise, leave me alone
To this day, I say you thank you mom
All I can do is laugh and say look at where I'm at now

UNCLE

As a kid, I would see you in my dreams

These vivid images seemed so real

If only I could move

My eyes just depicted your being

And I knew it was you...

Uncle...

You always have been around in different forms

Your presence always came through

I wish we could talk to each other now

And catch up on time we never had

We will some day...

DERRICK

Darkness came too early for you

Not by your choice

Your light was dimmed by the consequence of others

You forgave them, but it wasn't fair

I barely began to shine my light into this world

It's sad because I barely remember you

But, I know your lantern shines over me in the sky to keep the darkness

from coming in as long as you can

BRAIN DEAD

BOOGEYMAN

Every kid had a night light
Just like every kid had that recurring nightmare
Mine was the boogeyman
You know how the story goes...
My version was different
Soul snatcher was his superpower
Shang Tsung and him would go toe to toe
And it wasn't the cloaked, shadowy figure that we draw them up to be
It took many forms...
Childhood heroes, family members, friends
They would get too close to the point that they'll reach for me
I close my eyes...
And then in that moment, it's like everything stopped
Until I opened my eyes
Panting...sweating...freaked out

REGGIE JOHNSON

MRS. DORAN

This woman in any other sense would be considered a witch
Because what she did for me in Kindergarten was nothing short of magical
I was destined for intellectual destruction
They thought that I was at a disadvantage
Her tricks up her sleeve were her teachings that made her not give up on someone like me
Who would've known how much of an effect her witchcraft would have on me?
She gave me the gift of self-reliance
If I want something, I gotta go get it
She gave me the gift of intellect
She helped shape me into the person I am

BRAIN DEAD

BROKEN PROMISES

All throughout life
I've had people emptying hollow promises
No sink or tub could contain the watered-down excuses I've received and dealt with
And that's when I wipe my hands clean
I had to learn that I had one promise to keep to myself
And that was to never let myself down
If I want something I can go get it

REGGIE JOHNSON

NIGHTLIFE

Hot summer nights...
Meant everyone out on the town
Walking the streets of downtown
Looking for the party scene
Or just out for a random adventure
Or a planned birthday outing
Or an over the top VIP
We danced...
We fought...
We even threw up a few times
The summer brought out everyone
I miss those nights

BRAIN DEAD

FIRST LOVE

It was summer camp
Our hearts were Frankenstein
My heart wasn't with you and yours wasn't with me
But, we made it happen
Swimming though this relationship, yeah, I had to put some laps in
Now when I look back, I can't help but to start laughing
Our worlds weren't meant to mesh, it was never going to happen

REGGIE JOHNSON

GROWING UP

I was that kid that always got picked on
Could cry to the point of being pissed off
But, I didn't give them the satisfaction, didn't wanna get their rocks off
Didn't wanna be judged by what looks good on paper
Didn't wanna be scissored out by people that'll end up needing me later
Never liked Rock Paper Scissors, never ended in my favor
As I got older, I got wiser
Taught myself to kill them with kindness and add a little of malice
Being slicker than a savage, I drink humbleness from my chalice

BRAIN DEAD

LOCKET

The one gift you gave me
A locket with a heart in it
Every time I open it up to anyone
They get a look at the pain and sorrow you caused
It's like I can't shake the stigma of being an introvert for love
Because when I'm in it, I give you all of me
And it's sad the only thing I received from my previous relationships
were stupid symbols of how dumb I was to entertain feelings for you
One of you I almost loved
One I was sad to see end before it even got started
Hopefully this locket is magical enough to become a magnet instead of an omen
Give me that feeling that makes me feel wanted

REGGIE JOHNSON

DON'T SLEEP ON ME

(Inspired by Don't Sleep On Me by Ty Dolla $ign, Future & 24Hrs)

Don't sleep on me

Don't be the next one in the bunch

Yeah, I've been hungry to get to where I'm at, I'm taking all the lunch

Back in school, I relied heavy on my mental

Can't believe at age of five, they would predict I would be slow up in my mental

Wasn't up to par with the rest

So, my teacher trained me to get a hole in one

Surpassed all expectations and then I was one of the chosen one

Honor roll led to honor society

Then I noticed, there wasn't that many people of color in here besides me

Stuck out like an antenna

Everyone tuned into me

To put in all this hard work and I still have to fight to be seen

Funny how life took me

After people telling me, I wouldn't be good at reading and writing

Who knew the irony I would lead as it's my passion I'm abiding?

So, don't sleep on me

Because I'll make you have a nightmare

And make you dream you wouldn't have written me off and instead could've cared

BRAIN DEAD

THEN & NOW

Everyone in high school is divided into certain categories

The cool kids, the jocks, the geeks, the drama kids, student involved kids

Early on, I was just in my own category

I just kept my head into books

Then, my mom made me bust out of my extroverted shell and try extracurriculars

First, I tried basketball…

Conditioned and trained

It was more difficult than any video game I would ever play from beginning to end

And it seemed like I failed midway as my real-life game of NBA 2K ended at tryouts

I stood out for not fitting in to a classification

It was like taxonomy in a way

Then, I found a niche from an old summer pastime

Who knew rolling a ball down a lane, would turn into a hobby of mine for the next 16 years?

Bowling helped me realize that I don't need to care if I stand out

Let everyone look at me

MVP, Most Improved and 3 trophies later, I think I'm doing alright

REGGIE JOHNSON

NATIONAL HONOR SOCIETY

Bowling was just the first
Academic team, Spanish Club and Student Council would follow
But, it wouldn't be until one day in religion class
I would learn of the meaning behind being "tapped"
Taken out of class, the only thing I could think of is that I was in trouble
I would go upstairs to a room with other students and to my surprise it was a christening
"Welcome to the National Honor Society"
I guess putting my head into books all that time before extracurriculars paid off

EDIBLE

Edible

That's what I was told

Get you high on another level

No one was daring me to bold

Finally, I gave in

I would not know the roller coaster ride I just got in

I wasn't strapped in, checked if I was safe

I just dove in

And I could feel my mind getting to the top of the hill

Hysterical at this point like the funniest joke was just told

And when it came down, all systems were go

Mind overload commenced, eating one thing after the next

Racing a mile-a-minute trying to articulate everything that was happening around me as if there was a secretary in my mind just typing away to keep up

When I got home to my bed that night, the ride was over

My mind said "hope you enjoyed the ride, please come again"

I don't know how to feel...

Should I do it again?

It was fun...

Right?

REGGIE JOHNSON

SIP

At first sip, you feel the rush
Like a power up in a video game, it kicks in
You think, this is not too bad
I can drink another one of these
1 turns to 2
2 turns to 4
4 turns to I can't remember
Memories fade to black like the Jay Z documentary
My mental is like Show Me What You Got
On my Kingdom Come
And I'll be mad when morning comes
That first time, I stayed up most of the night
Tripping off my high and off the furniture near me
I just wanted everything to stop for a moment
Even cats made me paranoid
Somehow, this was the beginning of a pleasure, I chose not to avoid

COLLEGE

The first day of college was like the first day of kindergarten
Your parents drop you off, enter a new world of new beginnings
My mom was sad knowing her youngest was leaving the nest
I left a young bird and by the end came out an eagle
Full of wisdom, experiences, trials and tribulations
I could soar above anything
Nothing was going to shoot me down
Such an introverted kid, broke out of the shell and molded into adult
And to think, I wanted to stay at home
Best decision of my life

REGGIE JOHNSON

LOW

Senior year of college
I experienced my first form of low
Stress was at an all-time high
As if the roller coaster of emotion was at its peak, ready to take me down for a ride
I did and I let everything out
I felt alone, I felt defeated like Cloud when he lost Aerith
Apart of me felt lost
As I lost someone's trust
All from a series of stupid events
If I could take it back, I would
Maybe we'll all be better friends now

BRAIN DEAD

RAINY DAYS

Rain brings too many memories

The lazy days

The "catch up on TV" days

The strong and severe weather days

The days where you go down in the basement and wait till the storm pass days

The real life Jumanji days

Because we would get monsoons of rain strong enough to flood our house

Several times

Like a damn holding its threshold until it breaks

And we sit there for an instance in panic

And then, adrenaline rushes

Get the water out now and fast

And through this all

Rain is like an emotion

We feel it, we express it and we adapt to it

Can't let this rain on my parade

REGGIE JOHNSON

HEARTBROKEN

July 28th, 2009 was the last day my heart was intact
She enjoyed every minute of it
Watching it ooze out
Never had I felt so broken...
So low...
So defeated...
And I realize now, the effect that had on me
Crippled me...
Reluctance every time I find someone I like
I can be very open when it comes to being personable in a given situation
But with liking someone, I freeze sometimes

FEELS

I want this read aloud at my wedding
May it resonate in my exes
The two that could've had my heart
The three that I never pursued
But the one I give it all to
Never said I could count in order
But I should get my ducks in that way
I should get my feels in that way
I should take her heels off that way
Should actually make a deal with her so that way
Bet on love and not on red or black
Read this aloud at my wedding
Music to your ears to keep you off track

REGGIE JOHNSON

REGRET

I can say this
The one thing I regret saying aloud
Is the one thing my heart was trying to
I like you,
But you moved on and moved away

BRAIN DEAD

APOLOGY

I feel like you owe me an apology
For all them years ago that I was hoping for monogamy
Instead this situation leaves us to grow up and stand tall on some mahogany
But like the tree, I went out on a limb
No trophy because I was no competition to him
He Bobby, I'm Ricky; New Edition to him
And if it wasn't love, then why you made it feel that way
Never forget how I felt that day

DRUNK

Drunken nights

Preconceived notions of how tonight was supposed to go

Then it ended up turning out completely different

Or was it everything that she wanted

He was just trying to get lucky tonight

I was just trying to turn up and not expect much

They just wanted to have and smoke one up

These nights usually ended at Steak N Shake or IHOP

Till four, five or six in the morning

Then, we wake up a couple of hours later...

Probably doing the same thing tomorrow night

BRAIN DEAD

LET ME GO

Anger was born that day
As I let the headache subside
I got the courage to get up out of bed
To get up and move on
But it wasn't that easy as I thought
I reached for my phone and I see your text
"Just let me go"
Then, I reread over the texts I don't remember sending her last night
Then as I read them, bits and pieces start coming back to me
Until I can see the whole puzzle...
And then I throw my phone across the room...
How could she do this to me?

FRONTAL

"Our dopamine levels increase when we use all of the lobes together in sync and the possibilities become endless"

REGGIE JOHNSON

RUNNING WATER

The faucet runs...
Water rushes through the piping escaping rapidly
Melancholy in emotion how the motion mirrors your actions
And everything pours out
The pain, the agony, the sorrow
The defamation, the disappointment
The list goes on and on like the water
Whoever pays this bill must not give a damn
Just as you didn't because you showed no signs of stopping
Even when you began to ease up, the pressure was building up
Surprised the pipes didn't burst
Don't like seeing you when you're at your worst
The faucet stops...

NOBODY

(Inspired by Nobody by Jhene Aiko)

I have these moments
Where I don't need nobody
But, me and my family
Too many emotions thinking everyone is mad at me
Too many false starts and I'm the one getting the penalty
Like it's so detrimental to me
It's all of me or nothing
When I give them nothing, they always up to something
Always giving something and I don't get nothing
Maybe it's me being nice, maybe it's my personal strife
No one can compare
They just think I'm a black little rich kid
Bottling up the stress and I'm ready to pop a lid
Don't fit the norm, and I don't really care
I'm on my One Republic, I'll just have them stop and stare
So, you can take this…
With a grain of salt
Don't you ever attribute my differences to being my fault
Don't you ever think you could be in my shoes just because you can walk
And don't you ever think you know anything about me just because people can talk
And I don't need nobody

REGGIE JOHNSON

WINDOWS FEATURING MITCH GREEN

Windows My heart has become a place where strangers window shop my love You put your hands to the glass Instead of having me in your possession Pigment of your imagination, an interest becomes an obsession Obsession becomes consumption You want to try to love but unaware of the basic function All you see to me is a price tag You couldn't buy me love that lasts Just likes for the gram and fulfilling little tasks Next time you're by my window, ask the owner about us And I hope you don't respond, they'll never be an us

-Reggie Johnson

Transparent silhouette mocking mimic behind a bent muse. Motion music reflecting through. I see the true you, tapered and used; a circus act – callused conscious to lose. Brand new addiction. Brand new scars. Brand new demons to die by. There is an ocean of human gold behind this fragility of earshot dimension. Damaged dogmas shipwrecked to Cannibalism; an urban cataclysm. I say smear the face of man, and unravel the hide of salvation. We all belong in a Pith of space. Coddled, kept fevered – a second coming.

-Mitch Green

BRAIN DEAD

SEASONED

Expectations fall

Like leaves in the wind

Seasons change just as the mood swings

I can't keep up with it

I adapt by layering my thick skin that I've made over the years

Your wear your attitude on your face like the different colors of fall

Yellow for bright and happy

Red because of the rage from the wildfire in your eyes

Green for the envy you have towards everyone else

All before you know it, winter is here and everything you know has

fallen off, awaiting Spring to come again

Take that time to look over your actions and mistakes and hopefully

growth will come in the seasons to come

CONSTELLATION

Most of the world doesn't see stars like we used to
We're just days and confused from the whirlwind of chaos going on everyone around us
Leaving us helpless, weak and not knowing what to do to make a change
As I kid, I used to see shooting stars go by in shock and awe
Now, I hope those same stars shooting are not missiles leading a campaign of destruction
Stars don't shine like they used to in the world
Most of us need to start singing Twinkle Twinkle Little Star again like when we were young

BRAIN DEAD

B.O.N.E D.R.Y.

Busy trying to fix something that
Only you were putting effort into and
Now I look dumb thinking that we could
Ever see eye to eye

Deceived by glimpses of hope when
Really you were showing me how
You were all along

REGGIE JOHNSON

SHADOWS

The shadows stood together like trees in a rain forest
The common denominator is that they cast shade
They're too cool for me so in order to heat me up, they
create a united front against me
You want me lit, well give me a match and I'll watch it all
go down in flames
And once the roots dissolve
No photosynthesis can bring back anything from what
you've done
And I just have to go over, what seeds were planted to
make you end up this way

BRAIN DEAD

D.U.S.K.

Damn, after all this time
U still give me the
Same look that
Kills me as if I saw it for the first time

REGGIE JOHNSON

LOVE BUG FEATURING CLYDE HURLSTON

You ever find the someone
That you just click with
Not like you select them with a mouse on a computer screen
But that connection
Not disturbed by WiFi, we made that LAN connection
Steady...no buffering
A lot of people pop up advertising that they're the real thing and end up being just more spam in my life
Need to get rid of the trash
Reformat myself and stop dwelling in the past
I haven't found them yet...
-Reggie Johnson

It was on the information superhighway, that I was driving with no hands. Aiming to let all of the fabled chips, fall wherever they may land. But I confess the goddess riding next to me, had her hand upon the gears. And she was doing things well out of view, that could surely alleviate my fears. But with information coming through, as fast as I was known to drive. There are so many things that one could learn, that would help you feel alive. Then she climbed over into my seat, and slid down on the waiting part. Adrenaline was coursing through my veins, so now the race could truly start. Streamlining passions never felt, as the cables dawned over our speed. And every time she'd rise and fall, she felt all the RAM she'd need. But now the data's building up, and the cache is begging to explode. I was helpless to all of her charms, seems she deciphered my every code. I had no choice but to upload, my consciousness in streams. For control is a true, elusive beast, much like the ghost inside machines. She took it all and wore a smile, as if she transcended space and time. Knowing full well she programmed my heart, and was displayed inside my rhyme.
-Clyde Hurlston

BRAIN DEAD

DAWN'S BREAK

The earth awakens its eyelids from its slumber
Sleepyhead that awakens at different times throughout the year
I wonder does it like how sometimes in the time it is asleep, so many bad things occur out of its control?
I'm surprised the earth doesn't wake up each day crying from the nightmares that occurred in reality
The earth's vessel must be strong to endure these kind of night terrors
So, the next time you see dawn's break
Be thankful that we were able to see it again

STORM

I find peace when the raindrops splash on the windowsill
The lightning appears followed by thunder
These were the days for cartoons and cereal
The days of video games and being lazy
Just sitting up in bed not doing a damn thing
Because this rain is for such a finite moment
I want to enjoy it while it lasts

BRAIN DEAD

SKELETONS IN THE DARK

I'll howl at the moon
You'll cry at the sun
Whatever skeletons come it in the dark
Make for sadness in the light
Dig up my graveyard of deception
While you garden your crops with agony and despair
And while you enjoying seeing my thrillers in the night
I'll watch the melancholy unfold in front me

REGGIE JOHNSON

IT FOLLOWS

It follows...

Like a ghost in a scary movie you don't want to cover your eyes for

Suspense is killing you inside if only you could look it in the face

Unveil the truth, the mask, the costume, the facade...

Guilt...

It follows...

BRAIN DEAD

UNMASKED

Behind the mask
Is it who people want to see?
Is it necessary for us to move on?
Is it subliminal or critical?
Do we solve the mystery when we make that big reveal?
No amount of Scooby Snacks could make we wanna deal

REGGIE JOHNSON

SHIPWRECKED

Don't usually harbor feelings
But this relationship is just waiting
Waiting to set sail
So captain...
Are you ready to take off?
Because once we go on this journey, there's no turning back
I want to know that when/if this ship begins to sink
I want to know that you'll never let go
Titanic love

BRAIN DEAD

MOONLIT

I come alive in the night
Brain switches in to the creativity and the storytelling
Endorphins fire off like rockets
Heat seeking interesting stimuli to synapse the thoughts on to paper
All the way up, on a high not coming down
Only turning off when the moon goes down

REGGIE JOHNSON

AUTUMN

As the weather begins to change...
So does people's actions
The colors of emotion change like the leaves and when they fall, they lie at the waste side
Maybe a pumpkin spice latte could keep you levelheaded
Nothing's ever permanent in our time
Why not try to keep our feelings in check?
Sooner or later, it'll be winter and you'll be looking for that someone that'll warm you up
So, don't get left out in the cold

BRAIN DEAD

LIFELESS

Motionless...

Lifeless...

Emotionless...

Lifeless...

Have you ever seen water stand still?

No flow of current, no waves

Have you ever seen crows in the street?

Feathers everywhere like a deadly pillow fight happened under the street light

Have you ever been motionless? Lifeless?

REGGIE JOHNSON

OVERSTIMULATED FEATURING JEREMY TOLBERT
(inspired by Overstimulated by Jhene Aiko)

Stimuli The sensations from your temptations Got me on a high Gets that's why ecstasy has two meanings Two different usages yield the same feelings And now you got me feeling something else Is this what you wanted? Dress it all up to make it look nice, is this how you flaunt it? An overload of emotions Senses becoming chaotic causing all this commotion Overstimulated, sensory overloaded
-Reggie Johnson

Exhaustion compresses my lungs, leaving me near death. I believed we'd turn to ghosts on a bed surrounded by candles and the moonlight. Yet, it was all make believe. Instead you walked away leaving me hidden in the shadows of an alley, high from the poisonous pill and a needle stuck in my vein. Overloaded from these emotions and the liquid running just beneath my skin, sadly the ecstasy I feel from you has turned me black and blue.
-Jeremy Tolbert

BRAIN DEAD

PRAY

(Inspired by Pray by Sam Smith)

I've been young and stupid
Now I'm older and wiser
Been knocked out, got up with my gloves on
I'm a fighter
And no one is gonna keep me down
They can try to take my smile and turn it in to a frown
But I pray
I pray for the day
That I don't have to deal with adversity
And just embrace our diversity
Not worry about injustice
Unless I'm playing the video game
Pray for all of us to stop evil and disdain
Pray

REGGIE JOHNSON

MADE LOVE FIRST

(Inspired by Made Love First by Marc E. Bassy & Kehlani)

Before we got to the particulars
Should've had your body perpendicular
Not have used for expenditures
Money should've bought your love
Because my actions weren't enough
And now I'm just now calling your bluff
Ain't sweet, I figured you like it a little rough
We should've made love first
Got snake venom in your eyes
They poisoned me to my surprise
And when I finally realized
My Scooby Doo senses have already taken off your disguise

BRAIN DEAD

BODY TALK

(Inspired by Body Talk by Majid Jordan)

Playing games in the dark

We don't even speak

It's ok to be different

She says that she a freak

Only for me, me, me

Fa sho we la ti do

Practicing them notes, let's see how high can we go

Or how low can we go down on it

So flexible, how you make your body limbo

And you do it only for me

WITCHCRAFT

A dark mage you were

You were easy breezy in the wind, just like a Cover Girl

You electrified my life bringing excitement and thrill

You lit a fire under my ass when I would be down to make me become a better man

And all of that went out the window, when you brought water to my eyes

Everything you did got me out my element

Not even Kendrick's music could help

You expect me to find something similar to you in an app where we swipe left or right

Just give me back my heart and I'll try to be alright

BRAIN DEAD

TOO GOOD FOR GOODBYES

(Inspired by Too Good For Goodbyes by Sam Smith)

Too early for hellos
Led us to be too late for goodbyes
Too much invested our feelings too itemized
Lost count of how long I could go without caring
I just wanted to distance myself without being overbearing
That just made you want me more
And I'll take nothing less
What started out being good for us, turned out to be the best

REGGIE JOHNSON

CROWN FEATURING STANLEY JAMES II

Crown jewels dilapidated Glimmers of success reflect off the face Showing glimpses of accomplishments Being masked by weaknesses And the dirty rags pile up as I become a peasant As no one will pay attention or give a damn to what I have to say And that's when I have to make them do so Realize that these jewels are dull right now but these rubies will shine forever These rags will be expensive garments And it'll all be accomplished with these words

-Reggie Johnson

Her body moves in a way that sings to me She graced the stage with sheer perseverance She steps up to the mic with both eyes closed Perfect rotations as her curves slow wind in unison to the drums Her anatomy is a piece of art But all they could see was her crown tilted A black woman is what they saw Don't tell her that her crown is slightly titled Tell her to raise her head up young queen The masks she tends to wear Hide a different story in that she bores It was her slightest touch You see her father gave her that crown Told her to let no man dictate her value before he died She spoke her heart out

-Stanley James II

BRAIN DEAD

A SPECIAL THANKS TO EVERYONE INVOLVED ON THIS PROJECT
FOLLOW ALL OF THE WRITERS ON INSTAGRAM

I.WIMANA.C: @I_WIMANA_C
ANDRE WOODS: @A.D.WOODS
CLYDE HURLSTON: @ADEBTPAIDININK
JEREMY TOLBERT: @RUMBLERPOET54
MITCH GREEN: @MITCH_GRN
STANLEY JAMES II: @IAMSTAN6400

BECAUSE THE INK NEVER DRIES UP
FOLLOW ME ON MY SOCIAL MEDIA

FACEBOOK: @R.D.JOHNSON0
TWITTER: @R_D_JOHNSON
INSTAGRAM: @R.D.JOHNSON

www.ingramcontent.com/pod-product-compliance
Lightning Source LLC
Chambersburg PA
CBHW030529010526
44110CB00048B/949